Date D

FRIEND TO FRIEND

How you can help a friend through a problem

BY
J. DAVID STONE
LARRY KEEFAUVER

group BOOKS

BOX 481 ● LOVELAND, CO 80539

FRIEND TO FRIEND

Copyright ©1983 by J. David Stone and Larry Keefauver

Library of Congress Catalog No. 83-80942

ISBN 0936-664-11-8

Fourth Printing

CREDITS

Edited by Lee Sparks
Designed by Laurel Watson
Illustrations by Jean Curtiss

Scripture quotations are from the Revised Standard Version of the Bible, copyrighted 1946, 1952, ©1971, 1973. Used with permission.

Contents

Dedication

For Sissy Stone and Judy Keefauver, who
know how to be friends and who are friends
to us.

The authors would like to thank some very
special friends for their contributions to this
project: James Kolar, who first suggested a name
for the process as it developed through the Creative Youth Ministry Models workshops; Carol
Reinberger, for her devotion to listening skills
and care counseling techniques; Rose Mary
Miller, for spending many arduous hours typing
manuscripts and meeting deadlines; Laura Jean
Kendall, for her preliminary editing; all of the
Creative Models cadre, who have supported our
efforts; and finally to the hundreds of people
across the country who have attended our workshops over the years, who evaluated this process
and affirmed it as vital to their personal growth
and development.

Preface

I've spent too many years feeling frustrated when friends came to me for help and all I could do was listen and patronize. My help for a hurting friend amounted to phrases like these:

"Gee, that's too bad."

"Now, now, everything's going to be all right. Don't cry. Don't worry. It'll come out in the wash."

"Bless your heart and hang in there."

Sometimes I would jump in and simply tell them how to solve their problems. But this approach was disastrous. It cut the friend off at the problem's surface. And if the advice bombed, I was the one blamed for the failure. Instead of genuinely helping my friends I ended up adding to their problems!

In an effort to help my friends more effectively, I studied various counseling methods.[1] But no single approach really touched on all parts of a person's thoughts, feelings, actions and spirit. And I did not desire to become a professional counselor. So, eventually, I combined bits and pieces from several methods, combined those with my own ideas and experiences, and arrived at a concept I call the Friend-to-Friend Process.

The Friend-to-Friend Process is not a counseling method. It is a non-professional approach for use by anyone who really wants to help a friend through a problem. It is also a non-responsibility approach. You cannot be responsible for anyone else's life. You cannot presume to know the answers to a friend's problem. But you can help the hurting friend sort out his or her own solution to the problem. **Friend to Friend** teaches you how to help hurting friends sort through their thoughts, feelings and actions and guide them to focus on what needs to be done. This book will help you become a more trusted and valued friend. They expect you to help them. Chances are high that they will not go first to a professional counselor. They will go to you, a friend.

Let's understand from the start that the Friend-to-Friend Process is not to be used with people who have major psychological problems. The process is for "normal neurotics," people like you and me, who simply need help from time to time with easily-identified problems. We need to refer those who are beyond "normal neurosis" to professional counselors.

This process that you are about to learn may appear simplistic, almost casual, because it is easy to follow. That is why it is so important that you practice it and practice it some more. The more you practice the Friend-to-Friend Process, the more you will understand the human personality and how it works. You will also help your friends take responsibility for their own lives in a meaningful way. You will become a better friend for others and a friend for yourself.

—J. David Stone

CHAPTER 1

The Friend-to-Friend Process

Susan was a high school senior who came to see me about a "terrible problem" she was having with her boyfriend. She obviously had been weeping shortly before seeing me. Here's a transcript of our working through her problem:

SUSAN: I need to talk with you.

DAVE: Well, okay, come on in.

SUSAN: I'm having a terrible problem.

DAVE: What's the problem?

(She breaks down and cries.)

DAVE: Do you want to work on this problem?

SUSAN: That's why I'm here.

DAVE: Okay, here's the way we work on it. Susan, the first question is: What do you want for you?

SUSAN: I don't know.

DAVE: May I invite you to say you don't want to know?

SUSAN: But I really do want to know.

DAVE: Okay. Well, let me ask you that question again: What do you want for you?

SUSAN: I want a better relationship with my boyfriend.

DAVE: What are you feeling?

SUSAN: I feel he doesn't love me anymore.

DAVE: What is the emotion that you're feeling?

(I look at her and I see tears streaming down her face and I see that she's all flushed.)

DAVE: Is the emotion that you're feeling sadness?

SUSAN: Yes, it is sadness.

DAVE: What is the sadness?

SUSAN: The sadness is that I love him so much and I don't think we're ever going to be together again. He's told me he doesn't really love me.

DAVE: What are you doing to get a better relationship with your boyfriend?

SUSAN: I came to see you.

DAVE: What else are you doing?

SUSAN: I'm not doing anything.

DAVE: Okay, now go back to the first question: What do you want for you?

SUSAN: I want a better relationship.

DAVE: You can't answer it the same way; you have to have a different answer.

SUSAN: I guess I want to be my own person.

DAVE: You guess?

SUSAN: I want to be my own person.

DAVE: What's the emotion you're feeling?

(She begins to breathe hard and grit her teeth.)

DAVE: Are you feeling anger?

SUSAN: Yes.

DAVE: What's the anger?

SUSAN: The anger is that every time we're together it seems it's always at my house and all we do is watch television. We don't ever go anywhere. He doesn't take me out to eat or go to the movies or anything anymore. We watch television at my house and I fix him a sandwich or something.

DAVE: You want to tell me a little more about that anger?

(She talks about what that anger really is for a few moments.)

DAVE: What are you doing to be your own person?

(She shakes her head.)

DAVE: What do you want?

SUSAN: I want to feel clean again.

DAVE: What do you need to do?

SUSAN: I need to break up with him.

(I already knew; at least I suspected the answer. But I didn't know all the data she knew. And if she answered the question she's better off than she would be if I told her what she needed to do. In addition, what if I had been wrong? So I made her take responsibility for what she needed to do.)

DAVE: Will you do it?

SUSAN: I can't.

DAVE: May I invite you to experiment with saying "I *will* not" instead of "I *can* not"? What do you need to do?"

SUSAN: I need to break up with him.

DAVE: Will you do it?

SUSAN: I can't . . . I mean I will not . . . but I want to.

DAVE: What do you need to do?

SUSAN: I need to break up with him.

DAVE: Will you do it?

SUSAN: Yes, I will.

DAVE: When will you do it?

SUSAN: Tonight.

DAVE: Will you tell me how it turns out?

SUSAN: Yes.

DAVE: Okay.

(I reached out for her hand. We had a short prayer and she left the office.)

The conversation with Susan should have given you a few clues about the dynamics of the Friend-to-Friend Process. It is a non-professional,

non-responsibility approach for you to help a
friend through a problem. You are not a counselor. You are a friend. You do not solve the
friend's problems. You help your hurting friend
sort through his or her thoughts, feelings and actions so that your friend is able to take responsible action on the problem.

The Friend-to-Friend Process centers on the
systematic use of three simple questions:

1. "What do you want for you?"

2. "What are you feeling?"

3. "What are you doing (to get what you
want)?"

Each question, although simple, addresses
three profound levels of the human personality.[2]
The first question ("What do you want for
you?") addresses our thoughts (or, the cognitive).
The second question ("What are you feeling?")
addresses our emotions (or, the affective). The
third question ("What are you doing?") addresses our actions (or, the behavioral). Let me
illustrate these personality levels for you. (See illustration 1.)

On each of these levels, there are innumerable
data banks. Every thought we've had is recorded
on the thoughts level. Every emotion we've ex-
perienced is stored on the feelings level. And a
record of our behavior is recorded on the actions level.

The Friend-to-Friend Process pulls data from
each of these levels much like a computer
operator pushes buttons to draw data from the
memory banks. Each question serves as a "button," pulling up data from the different levels.
That data is sorted and evaluated. You have
more data on you inside of yourself than anyone
else. That's why we cringe when others try to

Illustration 1

Areas of Personality

Thoughts

This level (the cognitive) is what you are thinking, the intelligence you have, or "head" knowledge.

Feelings

This level (the affective) is the emotions level: what you are feeling about all this, what's happening inside, your emotional response.

Actions

This level (the behavioral) is elicited as a result of what you're thinking and what you're feeling. It is what you are doing, or what is going on in your life.

force *their* solutions on *our* problems. Forcing solutions on another person tells him or her, "You are worthless and not capable to make your own decisions." There is no way that a helping friend can possibly know all the data about another friend's problems.

The Friend-to-Friend Process takes this assumption seriously. Since only the hurting friend has all the data on a problem, the helping friend's task is to pull up the data systematically from the three levels of personality. We use "What do you want for you?" and "What are you feeling?" and "What are you doing (to get what you want)?" as dynamic tools for getting the hurting friend's data out in front. This focuses on the "big button": "What do you need to do?" Let's take a look at the questions in the Friend-to-Friend Process.

Thoughts
(cognitive level)

"What do you want for you?"

This question deals with our "head" knowledge. It is at this cognitive level that our thoughts are stored. By the time a hurting friend comes to you, chances are that he or she is rather confused about what he or she cognitively wants.

The most important thing to remember is to get right to the point with the hurting friend: "What do you want for you?" Many times the hurting friend will want to lay out a whole "glob" of background to the problem for you to decipher, to know where he or she "is coming from." *Do not allow him or her to do that!* As I stated before, there is no way to know all the data about your friend's problem. And chances are that the friend will carefully "edit" his or her statements to gain sympathy from you.

So the way to cut through all of that unnecessary background information is: "What do you want for you?" For example, a youth worker in Illinois came to me who had taken another position on the church staff. It was very hard for him, however, to give up control of the youth ministry and let the new person take over. He said, "Now let me set the background of my problem for you."

"You don't need to do that," I said.

"But wait," he said. "I've been with these kids a long time . . ."

"No, don't tell me any of that. Tell me, what do you want for you?"

We continued with the process and he worked out his own problem.

Feelings
(affective level)

"What are you feeling?"
(identify the emotion)

This question helps the hurting friend identify the emotions he or she is feeling as they relate to the problem. This level (the affective) is probably the most powerful in a person's life. When we surface our feelings we get closer to our true selves. Feelings are the closest things that make up the "real me."

Sometimes the hurting friend will dodge the question by not really identifying the emotion. For example, a hurting friend may respond to "What are you feeling?" with "I feel like my daughter doesn't love me anymore." That response does not identify an emotion. Follow it up with something like, "Yes, but what is the *emotion* you're feeling? Is it anger that you're feeling? sadness?"

Feelings in and of themselves are simply there. They are neither good nor bad. They must be dealt with honestly, however, because they are the most powerful and often most confusing part of the human personality.

Actions
(behavioral level)

*"What are you doing
(to get what you want)?"*

This question focuses in on what the hurting friend has been doing to solve the problem. "What are you doing (to get what you want)?" relies heavily on concepts developed in reality therapy. Without going into unnecessary detail, reality therapy says that talking about feelings is irrelevant unless those feelings are tied to behaviors that need to be changed.[3]

For our purposes, this question generally leads the hurting friend to admit that he or she is probably not doing much, if anything, about the problem. Pent-up guilt feelings often emerge as he or she admits that nothing is being done about the problem. But it is also a healthy process to "confess" one's failure in order to do something about the problem.

Usually a person will scramble to think of anything at all that he or she has done to solve the problem:

"Well, I'm praying."

"Well, I'm going to church."

"Well, I've done a little calling on the phone."

The way to cut through the smokescreen is to ask, "What else are you doing?" or "What else have you done?" Almost always, the answer ultimately will be:

"Nothing."

Do you see what has happened? The hurting friend has come to realize his or her thoughts, feelings and actions relating to the problem. Now we're ready to punch the "big button" in the Friend-to-Friend Process: "What do you need to do?"

Thoughts *(cognitive)*

Feelings *(affective)*

"What do you want for you?"

"What are you feeling?" (identify the emotion)

In the Friend-to-Friend Process, it is essential for you to adequately explore the first three questions' data before hitting the "big button." An equally important thing to remember is to instruct the hurting friend to answer the question differently each time it is asked.

Turn back to the beginning of this chapter to the interview with Susan. Note how the first three questions are asked in order several times. By requiring a different answer (especially to the first question), we delve deeper into the personality and find the real problem. It's like searching through Cracker Jack to find the

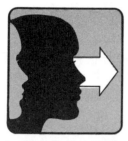

Actions *(behavioral)*

Integration of Thoughts
(feelings and actions)

**"What are you doing
(to get what you
want)?"**

**"What do you need
to do?"**

prize. The pertinent data (what the friend
honestly wants) begins to take shape and the unnecessary data is returned to the memory bank.
We focus in on the real problem, making the solution real and viable.

A frequently-asked question about the Friend-
to-Friend Process is: "Why is it necessary to
keep asking the same questions over and over?"
To the observer of the process, it seems so re-
dundant and bothersome. But to the hurting
friend, the questions are hard work! The hurting
friend must *work* to sort out the important data
from the unimportant data.

Another reason to ask the same questions several times is that often the problem presented is not the real problem. For example, in the conversation with Susan at the beginning of this chapter, she thought that she wanted a better relationship with her boyfriend when deep down she knew that she had to break up with him. We all tend to cover the real problem because it is often hurtful. The Friend-to-Friend Process provides a friend to the hurting person so that he or she is not alone when the real problem emerges. A hurting friend needs you to stand with him or her. You are an enabler, a resource.

With adolescents, a common response to these questions is, "I don't know." Before I used the Friend-to-Friend Process, I would play their game. "Oh come on, man," I'd say with my "hip" jive in full gear. "You know, sure you know. What do you want for you?"

"I don't know," he would say.

"Sure you do," I'd come back.

"No, I don't."

"Yes, you do."

We would go on in this dead-end dialogue until one of us gave up, usually me.

The Friend-to-Friend Process does not allow for repeated "I don't know." Since the friend must answer the questions differently each time, he or she is guided almost automatically to the real problem. You allow "I don't know" the first time through but not the second. For example:

"What do you want?"

"I don't know."

"Okay. What are you feeling?"

"I don't know."

"Okay. What are you doing?"

"I'm not doing anything."

"Let's go through the questions again. What do you want?"

"I don't know."

"No, you must answer it differently the second time."

"Oh . . . well . . . I want to be closer to my dad."

You see, by requiring different answers to the questions, the process has a built-in propellant that moves you on through the conversation.

How many times should you ask the set of three questions? My general guideline is to go through the questions, in order, three times. Often you'll need to ask them four or five times. I've occasionally needed to ask them only one time. Sometimes I've simply had to ask, "Are you in touch with what you need to do?"

"Yes," the friend responds.

"Okay, what do you need to do?"

"I need to call my friend Steve and tell him I'm sorry."

"Will you do that?"

"Yes, I will right now."

That friend, however, is the exception, not the rule. So go through them three or more times. In any case, you cannot go wrong. If you think you need to go through them again, go ahead. If you think you've gone through them too many times, there is usually no damage done. If anything, the friend has focused even more on the problem. If you think you've pushed the "big button" prematurely, simply go back to the first question: "What do you want for you?"

My experience in training people in the Friend-to-Friend Process has been that both the helping and hurting friend seem to know instinctively after a little practice when to push the "big button": "What do you need to do?" It is as though a spotlight floods the stage with bright light when this question is asked. The hurting friend is usually relieved because now he or she knows exactly what must be done to get what he or she wants. The friend is ready to take action on the problem.

Sometimes the hurting friend will set a wildly unrealistic goal in response to, "What do you need to do?" For example, a young adult was struggling with a vocational decision. She worked through thoughts, feelings and actions related to her problem: Should she continue working in a dead-end job at a health club or go to graduate school and prepare for a career in recreational therapy? She decided that what she needed to do was quit her job and go to graduate school. In that case, it seemed wise to explore a piece of that big goal: "What's one thing you need to do right now to get what you want?" She narrowed it down to: "I need to go to the college library and look through the universities' catalogs and write away for information on their programs." Now she had a realistic goal for herself.

A Few Follow-up Questions

Often in our lives we know exactly what needs to be done to solve a problem. We stumble, however, by not committing ourselves to *doing* what needs to be done. It is as if we draw up a detailed contract for the solution but never put our signatures on the dotted line. We need to follow through any decision we make or else our frustration merely increases. The following questions are the "follow-through" buttons in the Friend-to-Friend Process.

"Will you do it?" Once the friend has determined what he or she needs to do, a commitment must be made to do it. The friend must answer the question with either a "yes" or a "no." Other answers are prohibited. Often a friend will attempt a con: "I can't" or "I'll try." Face it, those translate ultimately to "no, I will not do what I need to do." And if a friend does say "no," your response must fit in the non-responsibility model of this process: "Okay, we're finished. See you later."

"When will you do it?" If your friend commits himself or herself to doing what needs to be done, continue following through the Friend-to-Friend Process with this question. The hurting friend then determines not only what needs to be done but also *when* he or she will do it.

"How will you do it?" This question acts as a catalyst for the friend to begin resourcing to solve the problem. Its purpose is to help your friend explore several ways to get help for the problem. Your response to the answer should be a simple nod or an "okay." Do not challenge the friend's ideas. Remember, it is not your problem and therefore not your responsibility to solve it.

"Will you let me know how it goes?" This question builds an accountability. We are generally more motivated to solve a problem if we feel a need to report the results of our efforts. This question commits a friend to report back to you after working through the problem. If the friend says "no" to the question, so be it. Do not twist

his or her arm for a "yes." Again, you are not responsible for the problem. And sometimes the friend will say "yes" but never tell you how it went. That's okay. Do not go to the friend at a later time and ask, "Hey, how come you never let me know what happened?" Respect your friend's right to solve his or her problems. An unsolicited demand for feedback tells your friend that you really don't trust him or her. They feel betrayed. So, if you can, forget the conversation and move on. You have fulfilled the expectations of the Friend-to-Friend Process.

CHAPTER 2

Putting the Friend-to-Friend Process to Work

A skeleton cannot walk unless it has all of the muscles, tendons and other necessary tissues. The previous chapter presented the "skeleton" of the Friend-to-Friend Process. This chapter will put "muscle" on the skeleton of this dynamic process. We will explain the setting, skills and procedure for transforming these paper-and-ink pages into a valuable skill that you will claim as your own and use effectively with your hurting friends. You will become the Friend-to-Friend Process in your own unique situation to your own special friends.

The Friend-to-Friend Process is not static. You may at times supplement the process with other skills and talents. I have found it helpful, however, to stay within the guidelines presented here.

The Hurting Friend Must Come to You

Sometimes we feel like reaching out to a hurting friend with unsolicited (and usually unwanted) "foolproof" advice for running his or her life. The Friend-to-Friend Process does not allow for this. Remember our commitment to non-responsibility for a friend's problem. You do not seek the friend out.

By the time a hurting friend comes to you, he or she already has an idea of what is the problem. The friend has been processing it long before coming to you. He or she doesn't automatically think, "Hey, I've got a problem." The friend comes to you for help in solving the problem. That's a great compliment! The person trusts you to listen with compassion, to enable him or her to sort through a "glob" of data and to direct him or her to a solution.

Sometimes a person's request for help is prefaced by a protective shield. Some call this shield a "cry for help." You can usually read a cry for help. You can often see it in their pleading eyes. Sometimes it takes the form of unusual behavior. For example, if someone unexpectedly calls you at 10:30 p.m. "just to talk," chances are good that the unusual behavior is a cry for help. The person is searching you out to see if he or she can trust you. If you can be trusted, the person will soon share the real reason for calling you: He or she needs a friend to help work through a problem.

Describe the Friend-to-Friend Process

Your first response to a person who seeks your friendship should be something like this: "Do you want to work on that problem?" By answering that question, the hurting friend initiates a contract with you to solve the problem, not simply talk about it.

After an affirmative answer to the question above, it is necessary for you to explain *briefly* the Friend-to-Friend Process. Succinctly tell your friend about the three levels of human personality and how you are going to ask him or her to answer three questions (differently each time) in order to focus on the real problem and what needs to be done about it. Allow your friend to stop the process at any time. For example: "Jane, you have agreed to work on a problem. What we're going to do is systematically probe the thoughts, feelings and actions related to the problem by asking you, 'What do you want for you?' and 'What are you feeling?' and 'What are you doing to get what you want?' We'll go through these questions a few times in that order. I want you to respond differently to each question the second and third times. You may tell me whatever you want to tell me, and you may stop the process any time you want. I will also confront any 'cons' (I will explain the cons shortly) you say. Ready? Okay, what do you want for you?"

It is important that the friend knows exactly what to expect from the beginning. Otherwise it can turn out to be a weird kind of game. I even write out the questions on a piece of paper or a blackboard as I explain the process to the friend. This also helps to keep the conversation on track.

Employ Good Listening Habits

Perhaps the strongest value in friendship is knowing that someone will be there for you to hear what you say and feel what you feel. The Friend-to-Friend Process does not require any mysterious or sophisticated listening skills. It does require, however, a friend who will develop some good listening habits. Let's quickly look at a few of these habits:

1. Crawl into the situation. This is called empathy. As your friend talks, work at understanding how he or she is feeling. Think, act and feel in their interest. It's much like listening to jazz music. You simply cannot hear jazz. It is much more than hearing the horns, woodwinds and so on. To really listen to jazz, you must lie down on the couch and close your eyes. You feel the beat. You imagine what might be going on inside those players. You get wrapped up in the music and let it take you away. It's the same kind of process when you empathize with a friend. You crawl into their thoughts, feelings and actions.

2. Maintain good eye contact. We do not hear only with our ears. We hear a great deal through our eyes. Eyes tell a person's story. If you want to know people, watch their eyes. That's why it is so important to keep good eye contact. Your minds mell together. Good eye contact lets your friend know you are really interested in what is being said. Your friend feels more secure.

3. Nod understanding. An excellent way to show understanding is a simple nod of your head. A nod tells your friend that you understand what has been said. But do not play "amateur psychologist" by nodding your head all the time. Your friend will pick up on your game and feel betrayed. So nod your head sincerely and appropriately.

4. Confront the "cons." Many times in the Friend-to-Friend Process, the hurting friend will attempt to "con" (confidence game playing) himself or herself or you. The friend will use con words and phrases like "I'll try," "I guess so," "maybe," "possibly," "sort of," "kind of," "I can't," etc. Quickly scan the conversation with Susan in the previous chapter, looking for the various cons she used and how I confronted them. When a friend uses a con word, immediately point it out. Do not allow the friend to con you or himself. One way to confront a con is to invite the person to say the word or phrase as it ultimately translates. For example:

DAVE: What do you need to do?

FRIEND: I need to call my dad and tell him I'm sorry.

DAVE: Will you do that?

FRIEND: I can't.

DAVE: May I invite you to say, "I will not"?

FRIEND: I will not.

DAVE: Okay. Well, good luck and see you later.

FRIEND: What do you mean?!!

The friend in this case eventually did call his father. But it was his decision. Not mine. So our task as helping friends is simply to confront the cons and allow the hurting friends to act on them as they choose.

Keep an Eye on Body Language

Most communicators agree that between 80 and 90 percent of communication is unrelated to the actual words we speak. Most of what is communicated is through tone of voice, posture, movements, eye contact and many other factors. Feelings especially are communicated through body language. For example, tears welling up in the eyes are almost-sure indicators of sadness. It is important that you maintain good eye contact in these situations. Allow them to cry. Do not "pat" them like a surrogate parent by saying something like, "Come on now, don't cry. Everything's gonna be all right now." Keep good eye contact and say, "Feel free to cry if you want to."

A few of the more common forms of body language to keep an eye out for are anger (teeth gritted, fists clenched, rubbing, clenched jaw, etc.), insecurity (arms folded, nervous laughter, wandering eyes, etc.), apathy (slurred words, sloppy posture, etc.) and sadness (tears, quivering voice, etc.). These are merely general forms of body language. They are not set-in-stone rules. It's up to you to watch and interpret your friend's unique body language.

Sit Directly in Front of Your Friend

The physical arrangement of chairs is vital to the Friend-to-Friend Process. I recommend that you sit knee-to-knee, face-to-face, nose-to-nose and eye-to-eye. Do not sit behind a desk or a table. You should sit close enough to touch your friend but far enough away so as not to invade the friend's private space (about 14 to 18 inches from the body).

This arrangement says a couple important things to the friend. First, it tells the friend you are interested in seriously working on the problem. Second, it tells your friend that you're involved intimately with him or her. You both are more able to hear and see each other.

Close the Conversation With Touch

After you have worked through the Friend-to-Friend Process, the conversation should be closed with an element of touch. People in business do this all the time after making an agreement: the handshake. Touch cements the decision. This is closure.

I suggest that you touch in whatever way is appropriate for you in each situation. Sometimes it may be a simple pat on the knee, or an embrace or a handshake. Here's a guideline for knowing the appropriate touch in each situation: Whatever has been the established level of touch in your relationship should be the level of touch that closes the conversation. Some levels are:

1. a slap on the back.   4. a "bear" hug.
2. a handshake.   5. a hug and a kiss.
3. a slight hug.

If your relationship is on a "2" level, then don't close the conversation on a "5"-level touch. Only you will know the appropriate level for you in that particular situation. Trust yourself at that point to know what to do.

Know When a Friend's Problem Requires Professional Help

If you discover in the Friend-to-Friend Process that you're dealing with someone other than a "normal neurotic," stop the conversation and re-

fer the person to a professional counselor. You'll
know right away usually when a problem is beyond your ability to help, e.g., a suicidal friend:

"What do you want?"

"I want to kill myself."

"What are you feeling?"

"Ultimate despair."

"What do you need to do?"

"I need to get myself out of this world!"

This is not a time to ask, "Will you do it?"
Rather, when you find a friend in any extreme
emotional condition, don't play this game with
him or her. And, discontinue the process if the
answers disagree with your values. At that point
say something like, "Hey, this is really out of my
league. I need to get some help. Would it be okay
with you if I recommend you to a friend of mine
who is a counselor who has training in ways
that will really help you?" And then, if your
friend will allow you, take that person by the
hand and lead him or her to the professional
counselor.

How do you know the marks of a good counselor? I would never recommend anybody to a
counselor I didn't know and trust. The best way
to find out about a counselor is to sit in on a
group session or in a one-to-one encounter. Any
worthy counselor will allow you to observe a
group therapy session. Or, simply spend an hour
getting to know the counselor. But never, under
any circumstances, recommend a counselor you
know nothing about.

Finally, ask the friend to keep in contact re-
garding the decision whether to seek professional help. This enhances the relationship and
lets the friend know you care.

CHAPTER 3

God's Presence in the Friend-to-Friend Process

Perhaps by now you are rather curious about the role of God in the Friend-to-Friend Process. It may appear that God has been left out somewhere along the process. But that's not the case at all. You see, God is not part of the process. He *is* the process. Let us illustrate:

Our understanding of the God we worship is that he is God of the whole person: thoughts, emotions and actions. Therefore God works at every level of human personality because he is God of everything. Even if a friend is able to get in touch with his or her thoughts, feelings and actions and knows what to do to solve a problem, from where does the *power* come to solve a problem? Jesus Christ.

We believe that the best way to show Christ's love to a hurting friend is simply to be there. Martin Marty suggests that the real meaning of "what a friend we have in Jesus" is "what a Jesus we have in a friend."[4] By being a friend in this process, we are the body of Christ, through his spirit, to a hurting friend. You and your friend will develop more than a relationship. You will, as Howard Clinebell says, *become* a relationship.[5] That's why it is not necessary to pound your Bible, point your finger and proclaim, "Here's what the Bible commands you to do, so you go do it!"

Instead, we encourage you to become an earthen vessel of God, pouring his love and spirit into another earthen vessel: your friend. You'll find yourself growing closer to God as you enable and encourage a friend. That's the paradox of faith: The more you give away of God's love, the more you receive.

As we've stated many times before, the Friend-to-Friend Process is a non-responsibility approach to helping a friend. This non-responsibility extends to the person's spirit. As we share God through the process, something will happen to you and the hurting friend. And we do not know exactly what will happen. But that's not our business. We are in the sales department.

God is the manager of the Holy Spirit. He is responsible for management. We are responsible to be faithful.

Perhaps the best way to illustrate God's presence in the Friend-to-Friend Process is to look briefly at Jesus' model of talking and relating to others who have problems. In many of the narratives about Jesus in the New Testament we see how he relates in very positive ways, meeting the needs of individuals without trying to manipulate or control them. For example, in John 5:1-18 we see the story of the paralytic at the pool of Bethzatha. First of all, Jesus notices the man. Then he speaks to him, and finally he asks him to take action on his own. This pattern is similar in other narratives about Jesus.

First, Jesus noticed and observed persons in need. This is so important in our relationships and friendships with others. Jesus had known that this man had been lying at the pool of Bethzatha for a long time. He had been hurting, he had been in need, and this was something that Jesus noticed. Jesus was very aware and in tune with the needs and feelings of others. If we are going to be friends to those around us, there are times when we must notice their needs. We need to be aware of the life situations of people. One of the most affirming acts we can do is to take the initiative to notice people's needs.

There are times when people will come to us with their concerns. They will tell us what their needs are. At other times, they will not say much, but non-verbally they will communicate deep needs in their lives. We can pick up on their non-verbal or destructive behaviors. A simple comment, such as, "I noticed you seem very low today" or "I noticed how quiet and reserved you've been lately," can help them open up. Noticing people, their behaviors, their voice tones and their facial expressions can put us in touch with their deep needs.

Jesus noticed the man lying at the pool. This wasn't the first time he had seen him there. This man had been lying there a long time. Jesus knew that. He took the initiative to become involved in helping this man solve his problem without telling him what was wrong with him or how he ought to act.

Jesus said something. Then he listened. Once we speak to another person, making him or her aware that we are concerned, the time comes to listen. Listening conveys warmth, understanding, empathy, friendship and concern for the other person. As another person speaks, our attention needs to be focused solely on that person, what he is saying, and how he is saying it. Jesus asked the man at the pool of Bethzatha the first question of our Friend-to-Friend Process. "Do you want to be healed?" Jesus asked, "What is it that you want?" Jesus was probing. "What needs to be done here? What do you want?"

The man answered not only the first question, "What do you want?" but also the second, "What are you feeling?" The paralytic let Jesus know not only that he wanted to be healed, but how he felt as well. The man said to Jesus, "Sir, I have no man to put me into the pool when the water is troubled; and while I am going another steps down before me." Can you hear his feelings in what he has said? There is frustration. There is despair. There is an urgency of need in this man's response. This sense of helplessness, perhaps even self-pity, is on the feeling level.

The man also answered the third question. He told Jesus what he has been doing about the problem. If Jesus had asked him, "What are you doing about it?" the man might well have said, "I haven't been able to do anything! I'm helpless!" If Jesus had recycled this whole thing, he might have again said, "What do you want? What do you really want? Do you want to be healed? If that is what you want, why have you been sitting here helplessly doing so little over the years?" Jesus came to the point quickly. He said directly to the man, "Rise, take up your pallet and walk." At once the man was healed; he took up his pallet and walked. The third question of our model comes to bear at this point: "What are you willing to do about your problem? What will you do?" Jesus gave the man a direct possibility. He could take up his bed and walk. "Will you do that?" Apparently the man did not say anything. He took action. He was willing right then and there to act upon a possibility that Jesus gave him.

Being a friend is the essence of being a Christian. God is there for us in Emmanuel, who is Jesus, the Christ. Jesus was there for the paralytic beside the pool at Bethzatha. We can be there for someone else. It takes some initiative and involvement to place ourselves there. Being there just for someone else takes the effort to notice them, to give them some of our time, to speak and listen with them, to enable them to see possibilities in their lives for solving their problems.

What we say to people who are hurting is often not as important as being a friend, being present with them, standing beside them as they struggle with their decisions and take positive action in their lives. God spoke to us in the past in the Old Testament or the Old Relationship or the Old Covenant. Yet to become more personally involved in our lives, to speak to us fully, his Word became a friend in the person of Jesus Christ.

As friends to others, we are a part of the Holy Spirit. We enable others, in turn, to know and experience the friendship of Jesus Christ.

CHAPTER 4

Case Studies of the Friend-to-Friend Process

Illustrations are necessary to enhance any thesis. The first three chapters covered the basics of the Friend-to-Friend Process, its procedure and its foundation in the Holy Spirit. This chapter features some case studies of the Friend-to-Friend Process at work helping real people solve real problems. I will clarify and comment on the process here and there in these case studies. As you read through them, keep the Friend-to-Friend Process in mind. You might even mark each "What do you want?" with a numeral 1; each "What are you feeling?" with a numeral 2; each "What are you doing?" with a numeral 3. Circle the con words. After finishing the case study, go through it again and focus on how the Friend-to-Friend Process worked in that particular case.

Case #1:
Tommy, a frustrated youth worker

This conversation took place in one of the Creative Youth Ministry Models workshops. I had explained the Friend-to-Friend Process and asked for a volunteer to come before the participants with a genuine problem needing the caring help of a friend.

DAVE: Tommy, I want you to pretend that there is a wall here and that there are just the two of us. Do you understand that I will ask several questions and that each time I ask the same question, you are to give a different answer? I am going to confront any cons that I feel you are throwing out. You can stop any time you want to. Are you in touch with what you want for you?

TOMMY: To gain a greater control over the youth and the staff situation in my church.

DAVE: What are you feeling?

TOMMY: A lot of anger and frustration.

DAVE: What is the frustration?

TOMMY: Mad because of several people going behind my back.

DAVE: What are you doing to get control over your youth ministry?

TOMMY: Just charging ahead and doing the things that need to be done.

DAVE: What do you want for you?

TOMMY: I don't want to be hampered in my job situation.

DAVE: What are you feeling?

TOMMY: I'm feeling alone.

DAVE: What's the aloneness?

(Tommy needed to identify the emotion.)

TOMMY: I feel like I'm trying to . . . I feel like I'm being forced to do it all on my own.

DAVE: You feel like you're being forced to do it on your own? What are you doing to keep from being alone?

TOMMY: Trying to encourage . . .

DAVE: That word try . . . I want to show you something. I want you to *try* to take this pen away from me. No, don't take it. I want you to *try* to. See, when you *try* to do something it usually means you're not doing it. Let me ask you again. What are you doing to keep from being alone in your work?

TOMMY: I don't know . . . I can't think of anything else other than what I've already said.

DAVE: What do you want for Tommy?

TOMMY: I want to get control of the situation.

DAVE: What are you feeling?

TOMMY: I am feeling incompleteness.

DAVE: What is your incompleteness?

TOMMY: I don't feel as though I belong. I feel like everyone is doing his own thing and leaving me out.

DAVE: What are you doing to overcome your incompleteness?

TOMMY: Nothing, really.

DAVE: Nothing. Really?

(Confront the con.)

TOMMY: Nothing.

DAVE: What do you need to do?

TOMMY: Establish some line of communication between myself and the staff person.

DAVE: Will you do it?

TOMMY: Yes.

DAVE: How will you do it?

TOMMY: I will go see him and explain how I have been feeling.

DAVE: What else will you do?

TOMMY: I will ask that we have some time together each week to "touch base."

DAVE: That is good work, Tommy! When will you do this?

TOMMY: Tomorrow morning!

DAVE: Great! Will you let me know how it comes out?

TOMMY: Sure.

(To close this contract, I shook his hand and embraced him.)

Case #2:

Ben, a teenager kicked out of home

Ben came into my office and he said, "Dave, I really need to talk with you." I could see he was frustrated and scared. I invited him to come in and talk.

BEN: I've got a terrible problem. I've gotta leave home.

DAVE: That is a bad problem. You're a high school junior and you've got to leave home.

BEN: My dad's told me I've got to get out. Told me to pack my stuff and get out! He's given me a week to do it and I don't know where I'm gonna go. I've really got a problem.

DAVE: Would you like to work on that problem?

BEN: That's why I'm here!

DAVE: Okay, sit down.

(We sat across from each other, knee-to-knee, eye-to-eye.)

DAVE: Now, I'm not a professional counselor. But this is a process that I use and if you'd like, we'll use this process and work through it. (I showed him the three questions.) I'll ask these three questions and each time you'll answer them differently. I'm going to confront the cons. You can stop the process any time you wish. What do you want, Ben?

BEN: I don't want to leave home.

DAVE: Yes, but what *do* you want?

BEN: Well, I want to stay home.

DAVE: Okay. What are you feeling?

BEN: I'm feeling all mixed up.

(Tears were beginning to well up in his eyes, an obvious sign of sadness.)

DAVE: Are you feeling sadness?

BEN: Yeah.

DAVE: What is the sadness?

BEN: The sadness is that my mom and dad yell at me all the time and I yell back at them and we never talk. We don't communicate at all. They want me to be someone I'm not and can't be.

(Ben attempted to blame his problem on his parents.)

DAVE: What are you doing to get what you want?

BEN: What do you mean?

DAVE: You said you wanted to stay home. What are you doing to stay home?

BEN: Nothing! Daddy told me I gotta get out of the house.

DAVE: What do you want?

BEN: I want to stay home.

DAVE: You've got to answer it differently.

BEN: Oh?

(I could just feel him struggling with that and going deeper into that cognitive level as he thought.)

BEN: Well, what I want is a better relationship with Mom and Dad, particularly with my dad.

DAVE: What are you feeling?

BEN: I feel like there isn't any relationship at all.

DAVE: What is the *emotion* you're feeling, Ben?

(Focus on the emotion.)

BEN: The emotion is that, the emotion is . . . my daddy doesn't love me.

DAVE: And what is the emotion? Is it sadness? anger?

BEN: I'm really mad about the way he has treated me. And I'm sad that he doesn't love me.

DAVE: And what are you doing to have a relationship?

(A flood of guilt suddenly drowned Ben because he realized he was doing nothing to better his situation. He wept several moments. Finally he gained control of himself.)

BEN: Nothing!

DAVE: What do you want?

BEN: I just want Daddy to love me and I want to love him.

DAVE: What do *you* want for *you*?

BEN: I want to love my daddy.

DAVE: What are you feeling?

BEN: Sadness.

DAVE: What's the sadness?

BEN: That I really love him and he doesn't know it.

DAVE: And what are you doing?

BEN: Nothing.

(You see, he brought up the correct information from each level. He was ready for the "big button.")

DAVE: Ben, what do you need to do?

BEN: I need to go home . . . Oh God, this is hard.

DAVE: Yes, I know. What do you need to do?

BEN: I need to go home and tell my daddy I'm sorry and ask for his forgiveness and tell him that I love him.

DAVE: Will you do that, Ben?

BEN: I can't.

DAVE: May I invite you to say, "I will not"?

BEN: Okay, I will not.

(What I wanted to say was, "Why not?!" I wanted to shake him! I could see exactly what he needed to do. I wanted to tell him but I held back. It was his problem, not mine.)

DAVE: What do you need to do?

BEN: I need to tell my daddy I'm sorry and that I love him.

DAVE: Will you do that?

BEN: No.

DAVE: Okay.

BEN: What do you mean, "okay"?

DAVE: Okay, we're done.

BEN: What do you mean?! I've come here for help!

DAVE: Do you want *me* to call your daddy and tell him you're sorry? And to tell him that you love him?

BEN: You can't do that.

DAVE: I know. What do you need to do?

BEN: I need to go see Dad and tell him I'm sorry and ask for forgiveness and tell him I love him.

DAVE: Will you do that?

BEN: I can't right now. I just can't.

DAVE: Okay.

(That's where we ended the transaction. I reached out and took his hand and that closed the contract. Remember: Touch is the best way to close any contract. Two days later, Ben called and said, "Dave, I need to talk to you. It's important! It's an emergency." He spoke rapidly and nervously. He came down to the office.)

BEN: Get the card! The one with the questions! Hurry!

(I reached over and got the card.)

BEN: Go over the questions! Hurry!

DAVE: What do you want?

BEN: No! Just go to the last one!

DAVE: Um, okay, what do you need to do?

BEN: I need to get up and go tell my father I'm sorry and ask him for forgiveness and tell him that I love him.

DAVE: Will you do it?

BEN: Yes!!

(He was gone! He had been dealing with the material for those two days and discovered in the first conversation what he needed to do. But he was not ready to do that. After two days of digesting that material, however, he realized what he needed to do. And it was his decision.)

Case #3:
Rachel, a woman whose mother was dying

This incredible experience happened the first time that I taught the Friend-to-Friend Process to a large group. There were 150 people in the workshop. We were in the ballroom of Chicago's O'Hare Hilton Hotel. I was getting more and more nervous. My knees were shaking. I was scared that the process would not be accepted by the audience, which was overloaded with leaders in Christian education and clinical pastoral education. Lots of credentials. I felt smaller and smaller. When I heard a tape recorder click on, I knew I was in trouble. I got that feeling: cotton mouth, perspiration and a naggy voice inside saying, "Man, what am I doing here?" But I went ahead and described, in a little detail, the Friend-to-Friend Process with the people. Several people raised eyebrows and coughed, a sure sign of skepticism. I finally decided that the best way to convince these people that it worked would have to be an example. I asked for a volunteer to help me demonstrate the Friend-to-Friend Process. A woman from the back of the ballroom came forward and sat down across from me. I explained the process briefly, told her I would confront the cons and that she could stop the process at any time.

DAVE: Now you understand what we're going to do. You want to tell me where you're from?

RACHEL: I'm from Louisiana originally. I live in Detroit now. I've been working there eight years.

DAVE: Are you in touch with something you want for yourself?

RACHEL: Yes.

DAVE: Okay, just tell me what you want for you.

RACHEL: I want to be close to my family.

(I thought, "Boy, this is a textbook case." I was afraid it was going to be something weird.)

DAVE: All right, what are you feeling?

RACHEL: Alienation.

DAVE: You're feeling apart?

RACHEL: Yes.

DAVE: What is that emotion of alienation? that feeling of being alienated?

RACHEL: Well, my family lives down in Jamestown, Louisiana and I live in Detroit and I haven't really seen them in over six years.

DAVE: You haven't really seen them?

(Confront the con.)

RACHEL: Well, I haven't seen them.

DAVE: What are you doing to get what you want—to have a closer relationship with your family?

RACHEL: Nothing.

DAVE: What do you want?

RACHEL: I want a closer relation . . .

DAVE: No, you have to answer it differently this time.

RACHEL: I want to be closer to my mother.

DAVE: What are you feeling?

(I noticed her eyes beginning to glaze over with tears.)

DAVE: Are you feeling sadness?

(She nodded her head.)

DAVE: What's the sadness?

RACHEL: The sadness is that Mother and I haven't talked in six years. We had a fight. She said she never wanted to see me again and I told her I never wanted to see her again.

DAVE: What are you doing to get closer to your mother?

RACHEL: Nothing.

DAVE: What do you want?

RACHEL: I want to get closer to her. I want to tell my mother . . . I want to tell my mother that I love her and I want her to tell me that she loves me.

DAVE: What is your sadness?

(I didn't have to ask her what she was feeling.)

RACHEL: The sadness is that she's in the hospital . . . and . . . I understand that she may not last much longer . . . and . . . I may never get to hold her or love her ever again.

DAVE: What are you doing?

RACHEL: Nothing.

DAVE: What do you need to do?

(She cried and cried. I let her cry until she got back in control.)

DAVE: What do you need to do?

RACHEL: I need to get up from here and go call my mother . . . tell her that I love her and ask her if I can come home.

DAVE: What's keeping you?

(I should have asked, "Will you do that?" But I was caught off guard, this being the first group presentation. She jumped up and ran out of the room! I jumped up to follow her but stopped myself: "Don't rescue her! Let her deal with her own problems!" I looked around at everybody and they were all about like I was—sitting on the edge of their seats, crying. She ran out of the door, crying all the way. I thought, "Well, one of these professional people will get up and go help her. Somebody's got compassion." Nobody moved; they just sat there, frozen. I remember doing the thing that most good educators do: I turned back around to the board, wiping my eyes, and went back over the questions. In a few moments, the door opened just in time to save me. As the door swung open, it smashed into a fire extinguisher. Everybody turned and looked. It was Rachel. She said: "I just called home and talked to my mother. I told her that I love her and she said she loves me, too, and to come on home. I'm leaving. I'm going home!" Then she left. Everybody gave her a standing ovation. Then, I turned to the crowd and said, "Now that's being a friend!")

CHAPTER 5

Your Turn

Now it is your turn to crawl into the Friend-to-Friend Process. You have read about the process and looked through a few case studies of it in action. In this chapter you'll read through a Friend-to-Friend conversation (part one) and then complete the exercises (part two) following the conversation.

Part One: The Conversation

This conversation was between two friends, both college students. The "friend" used the Friend-to-Friend Process with John, who needed to make some important decisions.

1) **JOHN:** I've got a tough decision that I have to make and I am having some problems. I don't know what to do and want to talk about it.

2) **FRIEND:** Okay. What do you want?

3) **JOHN:** I don't know.

4) **FRIEND:** You just said that you are working through some problems and decisions. Now, if

we are going to talk together, I want to take you through a process of asking you some questions and I am going to ask you what you want three different times and each time I want you to tell me in different words what it is that you really want. What do you want for you?

5) **JOHN:** I want to get out of this mess.

6) **FRIEND:** All right. What is the mess?

7) **JOHN:** Well, I really had a lot coming down a few weeks ago: My parents back home were hassling me about some poor grades and felt I shouldn't be seeing so much of my girlfriend. And, I have a major presentation to make in class in two weeks and have been staying up late trying to get everything done.

8) **FRIEND:** What are you feeling? What is the emotion?

9) **JOHN:** I am really depressed. I feel really low. I can't see enough of my girlfriend. She thinks we need to separate for a while and maybe date some other people. I am really upset and tired of this whole thing.

10) **FRIEND:** What are you doing? You look very downcast and slumped over.

11) **JOHN:** Well, I wrote her a letter telling her how much I loved her and I got this letter from her. Here, read it. And after I wrote the letter and got her letter, she says she loves me, but we shouldn't see each other for a while. I feel more depressed than ever.

12) **FRIEND:** What do you want?

13) **JOHN:** Well, I want to get back with my girlfriend. I really need her.

14) **FRIEND:** What are you feeling?

15) **JOHN:** I am lonely.

16) **FRIEND:** What is the loneliness?

17) **JOHN:** Well, she and I could really talk together and relate to each other and I felt really good. Sometimes I would get in my car and go for long rides and that would feel good. Then when I had to work through a lot of stuff, I could just talk to her. Now she doesn't even want to see me. I don't understand it.

18) **FRIEND:** You sound a little angry.

19) **JOHN:** Yeah, I am really mad at her. I don't understand why she is acting that way.

20) **FRIEND:** So you are feeling lonely? and angry?

21) **JOHN:** Yeah, I really am.

22) **FRIEND:** What are you doing? About being lonely and angry?

23) **JOHN:** Well, I am just sitting around. I don't feel like doing anything. I don't feel like studying. I've got this presentation that I am supposed to plan for and can't get anything done on it. I have so much reading and writing to do and no time to do it. And I have a test and some papers to pre-

pare for and nothing is getting done. I am really worried about it.

24) **FRIEND:** I have felt overwhelmed by all my work also at times. It's hard for me to get motivated to do something. What do you want?

25) **JOHN:** I just want to straighten things out and get out of this mess.

26) **FRIEND:** No, remember, you said that before and you agreed that you'd answer a little differently each time about what you wanted or needed.

27) **JOHN:** Oh, yeah.

28) **FRIEND:** So, what do you want?

29) **JOHN:** I want to feel better and get all the things done that I need to do. I don't know where to start.

30) **FRIEND:** What do you feel?

31) **JOHN:** I feel really confused.

32) **FRIEND:** What are you doing?

33) **JOHN:** I don't know. Nothing.

34) **FRIEND:** You can do something about it. What is *one thing* that you can do?

35) **JOHN:** Well, I have all this research that needs to be done for my presentation before the weekend is over.

36) **FRIEND:** And you are worried about when you are going to do it?

37) **JOHN:** Yeah.

38) **FRIEND:** Will you do the research?

39) **JOHN:** Yes.

40) **FRIEND:** When?

41) **JOHN:** Well, I can't tomorrow. I have to go some place. And Thursday night, there is a big activity at school.

42) **FRIEND:** I see. When will you study?

43) **JOHN:** Maybe Thursday after school since I can't see my girlfriend. I'll just go for a drive and then go home and sit around.

44) **FRIEND:** How much can you get done then?

45) **JOHN:** Oh, well I guess I could get most of it done then.

46) **FRIEND:** You guess? Can anyone help you?

47) **JOHN:** Yeah, there are a couple other people who might. There are some people in the course working in the same area. We could team up and cover a lot more areas of research than going it all alone.

48) **FRIEND:** Who are they?

49) **JOHN:** Well, Joan and Deann could help.

50) **FRIEND:** Will you ask them to help you?

51) **JOHN:** Oh, I guess so.

52) **FRIEND:** You guess?

53) **JOHN:** Sure.

54) **FRIEND:** When will you do it?

55) **JOHN:** Tomorrow when I see them in class.

56) **FRIEND:** That's great!

57) **JOHN:** Yeah, thanks . . . thanks.

58) **FRIEND:** What about your papers and your test?

59) **JOHN:** Well, I've pretty much planned out how I need to study for them.

60) **FRIEND:** Let's look at the plan together. (He discusses for a few minutes when his papers and test are due. They look at a reasonable study time frame and work out when is the best time to study for each one.) So, now you have worked out your schedule; will you do it?

61) **JOHN:** Yeah, I think I can get everything done.

62) **FRIEND:** You think?

63) **JOHN:** I can.

64) **FRIEND:** Great! What about your girlfriend? What will you do about her?

65) **JOHN:** Oh, I don't know.

66) **FRIEND:** What are you feeling?

67) **JOHN:** Depressed.

68) **FRIEND:** Are there other girls you could date?

69) **JOHN:** Oh, sure.

70) **FRIEND:** When will you date them?

71) **JOHN:** I don't know. I hadn't thought about it.

72) **FRIEND:** Sounds like there is not much chance of her seeing you for a while.

73) **JOHN:** No, there is not really any.

74) **FRIEND:** So you have chosen to be depressed and angry about it and do nothing.

75) **JOHN:** Yeah.

76) **FRIEND:** How long do you choose to be angry and depressed?

77) **JOHN:** Well, it's her decision to cool the relationship for a while.

78) **FRIEND:** Well, she has made her decision, but you are the one who is angry and depressed. Those are your feelings.

79) **JOHN:** Yeah.

80) **FRIEND:** How long will you be angry and depressed?

81) **JOHN:** I don't know.

82) **FRIEND:** What will you do about it?

83) **JOHN:** Well, I guess I don't have to be angry and depressed.

84) **FRIEND:** No, what else can you do?

85) **JOHN:** I can look for some more girls to date and start talking with some of them.

86) **FRIEND:** You could do that, sure. When will you?

87) **JOHN:** Well, I am not quite ready for that.

88) **FRIEND:** So how long are you going to be depressed?

89) **JOHN:** Oh, I think maybe two more weeks. (He laughs and then says . . .) After that, I will be able to find someone new to date.

(At the end of the conversation, they shook hands and decided on a time in a few days to get back together and briefly check signals on what had been discussed and how John's plans were going. They had a short prayer together and then departed.)

Part Two: Exercises

1. "What do you want?"

A. Listening

One of the basic communication skills is the ability to paraphrase what the other person is saying. This demonstrates that we are listening closely to what is being said. It also conveys understanding, empathy and caring for the other person.

EXERCISE:

Notice that the friend in statement 4 paraphrased what John said and then asked for a commitment to the process. Rewrite below how you might have paraphrased the presented need or want of John.

_____

_____

_____

B. Being There

There are those who need our friendship. These persons have needs and decisions to make. The willingness of the friend to talk about their problems and work on the process demonstrates a high commitment or motivation toward making a decision. John sought out someone he trusted to assist him in a decision. It is important that we notice that the friend does not jump in and solve the problem or give answers. The friend helps work through a decision-making process. All of us at times need others to listen to us and accept us.

EXERCISE:

Below, list five people you might ask to

listen to you:

1)_____

2)_____

3)_____

4)_____

5)_____

EXERCISE:

List persons who might come to you with problems, decisions or reflections and would need you to listen to them:

1)_____

2)_____

3)_____

4)_____

5)_____

RATIONALE:

The purpose of these lists is to point out how interdependent we are upon one another. We have people who nurture and listen to us as well as persons who need us to nurture them. If we do not have this support community, we need to seek persons who will listen to us and care for us. Without these nurturing persons, we will find it difficult to make some decisions. Without a support community, we often find ourselves lonely and depressed.

C. The Real Problem

It is very possible that the problem presented to us by another person is not the real problem. It may simply be a surface symptom. It was possible in the conversation with John to get completely sidetracked on his relationship with his girlfriend. There was another problem that surfaced. In statement 23, John revealed inadequate skills for managing time and coping with stress. He needed a workable plan or strategy to alleviate some of the pressure. This is why the friend asked at least three times, "What do you want?" John reflected on his needs and wants differently each time, enabling him to really see what was under the surface problem.

EXERCISE:

In the space below, reflect on your own experience at a time when you were struggling with an important decision or a difficult problem. Reflect on what the surface symptoms were and then go deeper and reflect on what was the real problem and not simply the superficial symptoms of the problem.

_____

_____

_____

D. Our Needs and Wants

Notice statement 28. For the third time, "What do you want?" is asked. We need to understand that in many instances, what we want is very close to what we need. According to some psychologists, we have a hierarchy of needs. Those needs range from the basic needs of food, shelter, clothing and survival, to relational and psychological needs (acceptance, love, affirmation and realizing our fullest potential).

EXERCISE:

Reflect for a moment on the needs and wants in your life right now. List all those things you need and want from the most basic, such as food, clothing, shelter, etc., to the most abstract, such as love, affirmation, etc.

_____

_____

_____

EXERCISE:

Look over the list and circle the most important needs in your life right now.

EXERCISE:

Reflecting on the needs listed above, which of those needs are not being met adequately? Put a check by each of the unmet needs.

EXERCISE:

If you want to move a step further and take some action ("What will you do about it?"), then put beside those needs persons' initials who might be able to help you find ways to meet those needs.

RATIONALE:

Statement 34 addressed a basic need. Notice that the statement is very affirming: "You can do something about it." This is often the most positive thing that we can say to persons. Persons usually have within them the resources and the ability through Christ to act and accomplish positive behaviors in their lives. But, what is the appropriate behavior? And then, will I act? There is a basic assumption behind the question, "What do you want?" Here it is:

WITH THE POWER OF GOD IN CHRIST, PEOPLE HAVE THE ABILITY TO GROW, THE OPPORTUNITY TO CHANGE AND THE

RESOURCES TO ACT CONSTRUCTIVELY.

2. "How do you feel?"

A. Mixed Feelings

We hold many feelings within ourselves at the same time. Those feelings may be contradictory. We might deeply care for someone, and at the same time be very angry with him or her. We might enjoy being with someone, but at another time, reject the person.

EXERCISE:

List below all the possible feelings a person might have: _____

_____

_____

EXERCISE:

Now go back over the list and put a plus sign by those feelings which are positive, and a minus sign by those which are negative. (For example, love, care, compassion and joy are positive feelings. Hate, hostility and anger are negative feelings.) After you have put an appropriate mark by each feeling, look at the balance between the two. Are you a person who thinks mostly about negative feelings, and therefore listed mostly negative feelings, or do you tend to be a more positive person, and therefore listed positive feelings?

RATIONALE:

Positive feelings often enable and motivate us to take action, whereas negative feelings often are obstacles to taking positive action toward solving our problems or making decisions.

B. Non-verbal Language

We also need to be aware that communication happens not only in a verbal way, but also non-verbally. Our body language, facial expressions, tone of voice, eye contact, etc., communicate feelings.

EXERCISE:
In the space below, describe depressed persons (the way they look and act).

_____

_____

_____

EXERCISE:
Now describe anxious or worried persons.

_____

_____

_____

RATIONALE:
Look over your descriptions. A depressed person very often has little emotion or enthusiasm in his or her voice. He or she may walk somewhat bent over and look down a great deal. The shoulders may be slumped.

On the other hand, the anxious person may talk rapidly and be nervously moving the hands or sitting on the edge of a seat while talking. The eyes might be widened with apprehension or even fear.

C. Feedback

When communicating with another person, check your perceptions and describe his or her behavior. In describing behavior, you can share with the other person how he or she comes across to you with body language and all the other non-verbals that you pick up. You might say, "You are speaking very fast and have a fearful look in your eyes and a nervous tone to your voice. Are you feeling anxious and upset?" The other person can then let you know whether your perception is correct.

EXERCISE:

Now go stand in front of a mirror or imagine you are standing in front of a mirror. Imagine in your mind a situation in which you invariably become angry. Think it over carefully and imagine that the person with whom you are angry is standing right behind the mirror and you are talking to him or her. Express your anger in words and in actions the way you would normally communicate anger. Watch your own behavior and listen to your voice. If possible, record your voice. Now in the space below write a description of all the things you saw and heard beyond the simple words that you spoke. _____

_____

_____

D. Self-disclosure

Another way you might relate to a friend is through self-disclosure. It is possible to share your own experience with your friend. This enables the friend to feel your empathy and realize that he or she is not the only one who has felt this way. For example, look at what John said in statement 15. The friend asked what the loneliness was in statement 16. Read the reply in statement 17. Notice that the friend in statement 18 was checking out the perception that John was angry. That perception was confirmed by John in statement 19. Another possible response might have been a self-disclosure, in which the friend might have revealed an experience of loneliness.

EXERCISE:
   In the space below, try this out yourself. Recall a situation in which you felt a kind of loneliness. In two or three sentences, describe your experience of that loneliness and practice self-disclosure. _____
_____
_____

3. "What are you doing?" and "What do you need to do?"

A. Action and Inaction
   "What are you doing?" enabled John to get in touch with reality. At this point, the reality was that John was not doing anything about his problem. Until John recognized what he *was doing* or *was not doing*, he could not realize the need for action.

EXERCISE:
   Look closely over the conversation between the friend and John. At what points in the conversation did John realize that he was not acting on his problem? List the statement numbers where that occurs. _____
_____

B. What Needs to Be Done?
   Once a person has realized that he or she is taking no real action for solving a problem or

making a decision, that insight can pave the way
for future action. The friend is grounded in the
assumption that through Christ a person can do
all things. With that assumption from Philippians
4, the friend then invites another person to explore possibilities for solving problems.

EXERCISE:

At what point in the conversation does the
friend move from "What are you doing?" to
thinking of concrete possibilities for future actions? _____

_____

C. Realistic Goals

There are a few principles here. The possibilities for action must be realistic and attain-
able. They are small steps toward accomplishing
a goal, not huge leaps. Notice that John was
asked to name specific steps for accomplishing
his goals.

EXERCISE:

Try this on yourself for a moment. Identify
and reflect on a problem or decision you face
right now. Then, in the space below, list 10 realistic steps you can take for solving this problem.

1) _____ 6) _____
2) _____ 7) _____
3) _____ 8) _____
4) _____ 9) _____
5) _____ 10) _____

Look back over your list. If you listed only
one or two items, you are setting yourself up
to fail. Often it takes a long list of steps before

a problem can be solved. We often list impossible solutions to our problem at the top of the list. Since our list is short, and we only try impossible solutions at times, we are doomed to fail. The ninth or tenth item on the list may have to be executed before solving a problem.

RATIONALE:

In discussing the possibilities with a friend, you might also enable the person to see that he or she is not alone in this. You are there through the conversation, through prayer, through a concrete expression of support like a hug or a handshake, and through future availability.

4. The Cons

A. Avoidance

One way the person facing a decision or a problem seeks to con himself or herself and others is through avoidance. In this con, the person with the problem believes a problem may go away or solve itself if it is avoided.

EXERCISE:

Look over the interview and see if you can find this con. Write the statement numbers here:

_____

_____

_____

B. Blaming Others

Another con is the refusal to accept responsibility for one's own feelings. We blame others for the way we feel or the circumstances in which we find ourselves.

EXERCISE:

Find statements in which John blames others for his problem. Write the numbers here:

_____

_____

_____

5. The Power of God

Due to low self-esteem and past failures, it is difficult for us to believe, at times, that we can do something with the power of God about our problems. Listed below are a number of texts that describe God's positive power in our lives for solving problems and making constructive decisions.

EXERCISE:

On the line following each text, write an attitude that will positively adapt this scripture to your life. We have done the first one for you, as an example:

"I can do all things in him who strengthens me." (Philippians 4:13)

Attitude: Through Christ I can accomplish anything.

"Rejoice in the Lord always; again I will say, Rejoice." (Philippians 4:4)

Attitude: _____

_____

"This is the day which the Lord has made; let us rejoice and be glad in it." (Psalm 118:24)

Attitude: _____

_____

"In returning and rest you shall be saved; in quietness and in trust shall be your strength." (Isaiah 30:15)

Attitude: _____

_____

"Therefore do not be anxious about tomorrow, for tomorrow will be anxious for itself. Let the day's own trouble be sufficient for the day." (Matthew 6:34)

Attitude: _____

_____

CHAPTER 6

How to Help Yourself Through a Problem

The Friend-to-Friend Process is by nature a one-on-one encounter between a hurting friend and a helping friend. I realize, however, that there are times when a friend simply is not there to help. In those times the hurting friend may need to draw as much as he or she can from personal resources to begin solving a problem.

Mary John Dye, who attended one of our workshops, found herself alone with a problem shortly after learning the Friend-to-Friend Process. She did not have a friend at that particular time to turn to for help. So she became her own friend by drawing up a prototype of the How-to-Help-Yourself Worksheet illustrated on the following page. This worksheet allows you to adapt the Friend-to-Friend Process for your personal use. Simply write the answers to the questions in the spaces. Start with the first question and work through each one.

Keep in mind that this worksheet is *not* a substitute for the two-person encounter of the Friend-to-Friend Process. The worksheet is merely a supplement that you will find helpful from time to time.

THE HOW-TO-HELP-YOURSELF WORKSHEET

	1st time	2nd time	3rd time
1. What do I want for me?			
2. What am I feeling? (identify the emotion)			
3. What am I doing (to get what I want)**?**			

4. What do I need to do?	
5. Will I do it? (circle one answer)	YES NO (If yes, go to the next question.)
6. When will I do it?	
7. How will I do it?	
8. Can I get help?	YES NO (If yes, where and from whom?)

Go back and underline all con words. Rewrite answers to the questions by confronting and omitting these con words.

CHAPTER 7

A Final Word

When a relationship is established, then broken, there is hurt. When a person reaches out to another, but is rejected, there is hurt. We hurt because our strongest longing is *to belong*—belong to a friend, to a community, to the body of Christ. The Friend-to-Friend Process helps the hurting person *belong*. By being a friend to a hurting friend, we tell him or her *by our presence*: "I want to help you belong. I will go with you below the surface of a problem and be with you as you discover ways to belong, to be healed. I am not able to solve your problems. But I am your friend. And I'm here for you."

The Friend-to-Friend Process is not foolproof. It will not work in every situation. But it will work in incredible and powerful ways with your hurting friends. The Friend-to-Friend Process will transform you into a better friend as you help others take action on their problems and responsibility for their lives.

Notes

[1] I attended workshops and classes in transactional analysis, reflective counseling, behavior modification, reality therapy, and other therapy methods.

[2] See Abraham Maslow's hierarchy of needs in **Toward a Psychology of Being** (Princeton: Van Nostrand Reinhold, 1968).

[3] Naomi Glasser, ed., **How People Are Helped Through Reality Therapy** (New York: Harper and Row, 1980).

[4] Martin E. Marty, **Friendship** (Allen, Texas: Argus Communications, 1980).

[5] Howard Clinebell, **Growth Counseling** (Nashville: Abingdon, 1979).

The Friend-to-Friend Card

Take the Friend-to-Friend Process wherever you go. Carry the Friend-to-Friend card. You will never know exactly when a hurting friend will need you. Cut out the two sides of the card below. Put the blank sides back-to-back and have the two pieces laminated (look under "laminations" in the Yellow Pages). It should cost about $1 to have the card laminated. Then put your Friend-to-Friend card in your wallet. It will be your instant reference to the Friend-to-Friend Process.

The Friend-to-Friend Process

Step One: Explain the process.

Step Two: Ask the first three questions in order:
1. What do you want for you?
2. What are you feeling? (identify the emotion)
3. What are you doing (to get what you want)? (Repeat the process as necessary, usually 3 times.)

Step Three: Push the "big button": What do you need to do?

(side one)

Step Four: Ask follow-up questions:
1. Will you do it?
2. When will you do it?
3. How will you do it?
4. Will you let me know how it goes?

Step Five: Close the conversation with prayer, a handshake, a hug, etc.

Note: Confront the cons throughout the process.

From:
Friend to Friend, Group Books, Loveland, CO 80539.

OTHER BOOKS FROM GROUP BOOKS

THE BIBLE CREATIVE: THE GOSPEL OF JOHN, by Dennis Benson. The first volume of Benson's creative commentary, study ideas and preaching clues from the Bible. Benson offers hundreds of ideas for helping youth and adults experience the messages of the Gospel of John. Hardbound. $14.95.

HARD TIMES CATALOG FOR YOUTH MINISTRY, by Marilyn and Dennis Benson. Hundreds of low-cost and no-cost ideas for programs, projects, meetings and activities. $14.95.

THE BASIC ENCYCLOPEDIA FOR YOUTH MINISTRY, by Dennis Benson and Bill Wolfe. Answers, ideas, encouragement and inspiration for 230 youth ministry questions and problems. A handy reference. Hardbound. $15.95.

THE GROUP RETREAT BOOK, by Arlo Reichter. This is *the* resource for start-to-finish retreat planning, execution and evaluation . . . plus 34 ready-to-use retreat outlines. 400 pages. $15.95.

THE YOUTH GROUP HOW-TO BOOK, detailed instructions and models for 66 practical projects and programs to help you build a better group. $14.95.

YOUTH GROUP TRAVEL DIRECTORY, a nationwide listing of churches that offer lodging and hospitality to traveling groups at little or no cost. Plus . . . practical advice for trip planning. $7.95.

PEW PEEVES, a humorous look at all those little things that drive you crazy in church. $3.95.

THE BEST OF TRY THIS ONE, a fun collection of games, crowdbreakers and programs from GROUP Magazine's "Try This One" section. $5.95.

MORE . . . TRY THIS ONE, a bonanza of youth group ideas—crowdbreakers, stunts, games, discussions and fund raisers. $5.95.

TRY THIS ONE . . . TOO, the newest in this popular series. Scores of creative youth ministry ideas. $5.95.

Box 481 • Loveland, CO 80539